REPORTING
LIVE

PAIRED:

Two reporters in the line of fire. Sonia Nazario followed migrant kids on a dangerous journey through Central America and Mexico. Sebastian Junger dodged bullets in the deadly mountains of Afghanistan.

"Can you imagine leaving everything you know—
your language, your culture, your friends and
family—to strike out somewhere new? When you
see that up close, see what these people are willing
to sacrifice to obtain the freedom and opportunity
we take for granted every day, well, that's an
incredible level of hopefulness."

Sonia Nazario

"Courage is love—maybe the ultimate expression of love: I would rather risk my life than watch you lose your life. That's a very intense statement and every single soldier up there felt that way about everyone else—even guys they didn't like."

Sebastian Junger

Photographs © 2011: AP Images: 100 (Jim Cooper), 27 (German Garcia), 81 (David Guttenfelder); Chris Fortuna: back cover left, 3 left; Dallas Observer/© 2007 Jennifer Szymaszek: 10, 14; Getty Images: 54 (John Moore), 86 (Scott Nelson), 73 (Mike Persson/AFP); Los Angeles Times/© 2002 Don Bartletti: 18, 28, 32, 41, 47, 49; Panos Pictures: 61 (Adam Dean), back cover right, 3 right, 58, 63, 79, 85 (Tim A. Hetherington), 68 (Teun Voeten); Peter Colombo, President of the Hummer Club of Rochester, NY/ HYPERLINK "http://www.hummercor.com" www.hummercor.com: 93); Polaris Images/Giancarlo Ceraudo/Grazia Neri: 20; Random House, Inc.: 52 (Book Cover from *Enrique's Journey*, by Sonia Nazario); Reuters/Omar Sobhani: cover; Courtesy of Sonia Nazario: 44; Stew Milne: 94; Courtesy of U.S. Army Photo: 76.

Illustrations by CCI: 36, 65.

Library of Congress Cataloging-in-Publication Data

DiConsiglio, John.
Reporting live / John DiConsiglio.
p. cm. — (On the record)
Includes bibliographical references and index.
ISBN-13: 978-0-531-22552-3 (alk. paper)
ISBN-10: 0-531-22552-6 (alk. paper)
1. Journalism—Political aspects—United States—Juvenile literature.
2. War—Press coverage—United States—Juvenile literature. 3.
Nazario, Sonia—Juvenile literature. 4. Illegal aliens—Press
coverage—United States—Juvenile literature. 5. Immigrant
children—Press Coverage—United States—Juvenile literature. 6.
Junger, Sebastian—Juvenile literature. 7. Afghan War, 2001—Press
coverage—Juvenile literature. I. Title.
PN4888.P6D53 2011
302.230973—dc22

2010041900

Tod Olson, Series Editor
Marie O'Neill, Creative Director
Curriculum Concepts International, Production

REPORTING LIVE

Some people will risk their
lives to get the story.

John DiConsiglio

Contents

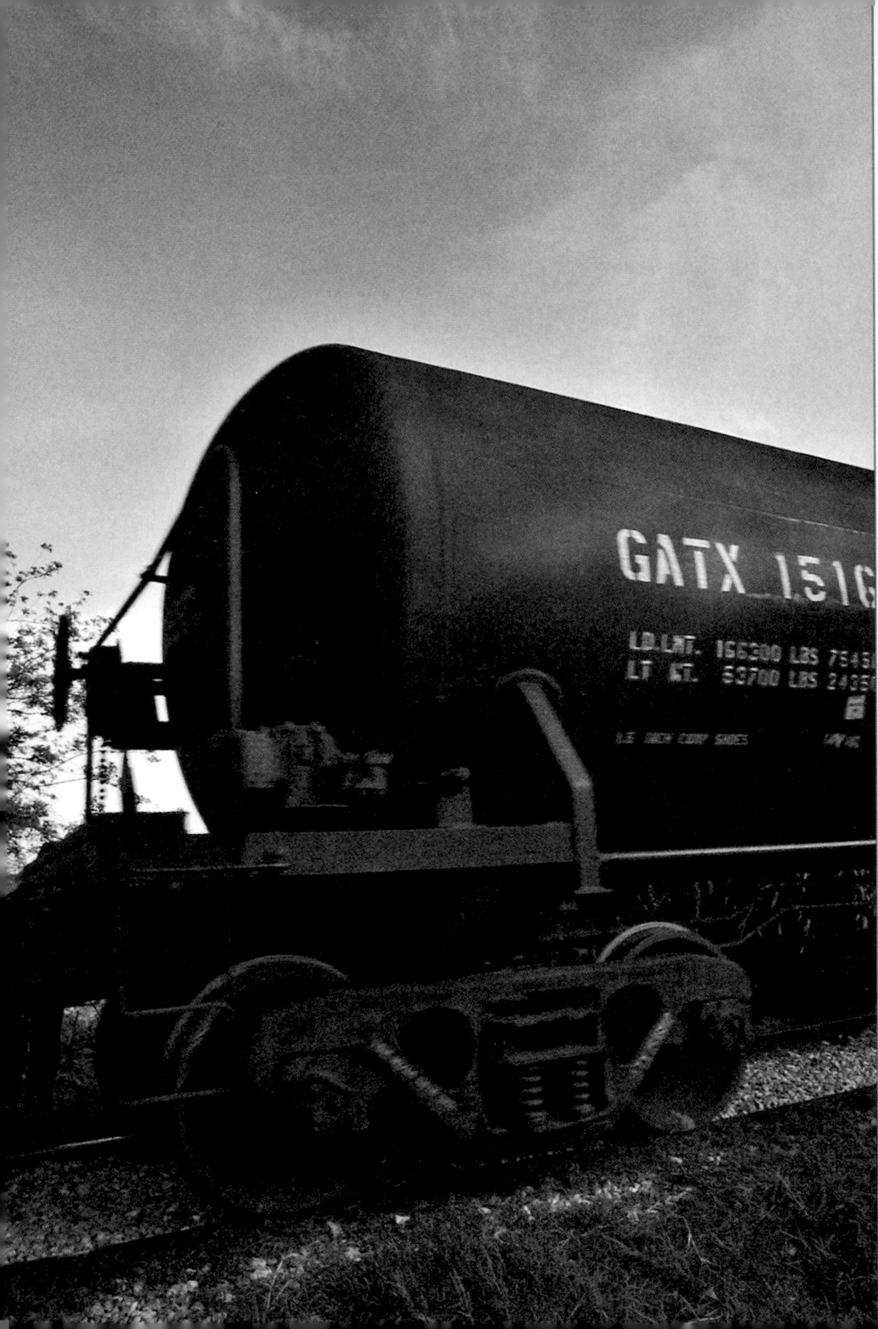
GATX 151
LD.LMT. 156300 LBS
LT WT. 63700 LBS

TRAIN OF DEATH

Every year, tens of thousands of kids leave
their homes in Central America, hoping to find
their parents in the United States. They make
their way north, dodging drug gangs, thieves,
and corrupt police. Sonia Nazario risked her
life to tell their story.

1
El Norte

Sonia Nazario clings to the top of an old freight train. Its wheels rattle along the tracks below. Rain slashes across her face. Lightning cuts through the Mexican night.

In the flashes of light, Nazario glimpses her fellow travelers. They are boys in their early teens with wide eyes and hungry faces. A few are missing arms or legs. Some bear scars from machete blades. All of them hold tight to the guardrails, balancing as the train rumbles through the darkness.

Every year, thousands of Central American migrants ride freight trains across Mexico on their way to the United States. The journey is so dangerous that the rail line is known as "the Train of Death."

The boys are desperately poor travelers on a long and dangerous journey. They have left their homes in Central American countries such as Honduras and Guatemala. Their destination is the United States. Most of them are trying to join parents who left to find a better life in the place they call *el norte*, or "the North." Each year, 50,000 of them reach their goal. Many more will never complete the journey.

The train they are riding is so dangerous it is nicknamed *el tren de la muerte*—the Train of Death. Gangsters, thieves, and corrupt policemen prowl the tracks, looking for easy prey. Many kids are robbed and beaten during their journey. Some are snatched from the trains—never to be seen again. Others fall off and are sucked under the grinding wheels.

Given the dangers, Nazario could be forgiven for wondering, *What am I doing here?*

In 2000, when Nazario boarded the Train of Death, she was a 39-year-old reporter for the *Los Angeles Times.* She wanted to tell the story of the migrant kids—and she wanted to get it right. "I wanted to put the reader on top of the train with these kids," she says. "I wanted to make people feel like they were riding with them. The only way to do that was to be there myself."

One boy in particular captured Nazario's imagination. She met Enrique in the middle of his journey from Honduras to the United States. He had already tried seven times to join his mother in North Carolina. He was risking everything to make the eighth attempt succeed.

On that hot summer night in 2000, Nazario was risking her own life to retrace Enrique's steps. She squinted into the trees that lined the tracks. Was that a gun muzzle between the bushes? Were gangsters about to attack the train? Nazario heard a shout from a distant car. *"Rama! Rama!"* Her mind raced to translate the word. *Rama?* Branch!

Suddenly, a tree branch struck her face. It knocked her over the edge of the train. As she fell toward the track, she grabbed a side rail just in time. She felt the sucking wind from the wheels below her pulling at her legs. She was just a few feet from falling to her death.

In the dark, she saw shadows of children running across the top of the freight car.

Riders on the Train of Death duck to avoid tree branches. Nazario almost fell to her death when a branch hit her in the face.

She heard voices yelling in Spanish. Hands reached over the side to her.

With the help of several boys, Nazario lifted herself to the top of the train. She lay on her stomach, panting and holding back tears. As the kids tried to calm her, she sobbed. Maybe, she thought, this trip had been a terrible mistake.

A woman views a memorial to the victims of Argentina's "Dirty War." From 1976 to 1983, the government ordered the killing of as many as 30,000 people. Nazario's family left Argentina to escape the violence.

2
Blood on the Streets

The Train of Death wasn't Nazario's first brush with danger. Since her teenage years, she has been drawn to stories of people living in poverty and violence.

Nazario grew up in Kansas, but her parents came from Argentina. When Sonia was 14, her father died of a heart attack. Her mother took Sonia, her sister, and her twin brothers back to Argentina to live with family.

At the time, Argentina was in the middle of a crisis known as the "Dirty War." The army seized control of the country and set up a dictatorship. Then it cracked down on its critics, killing as many as 30,000 people.

Nazario recalls walking with her mother along a bloodstained sidewalk. "I asked what happened and my mom said that two people were killed there," Nazario says. "She said they were murdered because they were journalists and they were trying to tell the truth.

"At that moment, my teenage mind knew I wanted to be a reporter," Nazario recalls. "I wanted to write about what was happening in places like Argentina. These were stories the world needed to know."

To escape the violence, Nazario's mother moved the family back to Kansas. In high school, Nazario worked as a waitress. Her mother struggled to earn a living as a seamstress and a cook. Nazario's good grades led her to Williams College in Massachusetts. There, she says, "I was one of maybe ten Hispanics on the whole campus."

After college, Nazario went to work as a reporter. She wrote about "forgotten people"—drug addicts, the homeless, people with AIDS. And she perfected the "fly on the wall" style that became her hallmark. For a series on drugs, she spent months following a heroin-addicted mother and her three-year-old daughter. She came home each night covered in fleas and smelling like urine. Her husband made her change clothes in the garage.

Nazario learned about the migrants' journey in the late 1990s. She sat down one day to talk with her housekeeper, Maria del Carmen Ferrez. Carmen told Nazario that she had four children in Guatemala. She hadn't seen them in 12 years. One of them was an infant when she left.

Nazario was stunned. How could a mother leave her children behind to come to a strange country?

Choking back tears, Carmen told Nazario the full story. In Guatemala, her husband had deserted her for another woman, leaving the family in poverty. Some days she had nothing to feed her kids. She gave them glasses of water with a teaspoon of sugar. At night, she made them sleep face down to quiet their growling stomachs.

Carmen decided that she needed to leave to provide a future for her family. She made it to California. She earned enough to send money and clothes back to her family. But bringing her kids to the U.S. proved to be nearly impossible.

The U.S. takes in more than 1,000,000 legal immigrants annually. No other country in the world accepts anywhere near as many immigrants. But the law favors three categories of people: skilled workers with a job waiting for them, people with family living legally in the U.S., and political refugees who are persecuted in their home countries.

Millions of other people know they'll never get permission to come to the U.S. Every year, about half a million of them make the trip illegally. Carmen's teenaged son became one of these illegal immigrants. He hitchhiked through Guatemala and Mexico. He begged for food and ran from bandits. Eventually he found his way to his mother's door.

"As she spoke, I felt the hairs on my arm rise," Nazario says. "It was chilling. I felt I had to tell the story of these boys. It was the kind of story I became a journalist to tell."

These immigrants have paid two smugglers to help them cross the Rio Grande. Illegal immigrants to the United States often cross the river from Nuevo Laredo, Mexico, into Texas.

Riders on the Train of Death are often captured and detained. The teenagers in this jail in Chiapas, Mexico, will be deported to Guatemala.

Nazario planned to research her story by living like a migrant child. But she knew her limitations. She couldn't trail one boy for the entire 2,000-mile route. There was no way she could keep up with a teenager on such a dangerous journey.

Instead, Nazario searched for someone who had already made the trip. She called churches and shelters that harbored lost boys. She went to immigration detention centers. Kids at the detention centers had been arrested on the way to the United States. They were waiting to be sent back to their home countries.

As she interviewed children, Nazario was stunned by their stories. One 11-year-old boy had seen a band of gangsters hop a train, high on crack. The thugs snatched a young girl and threw her off the train, killing her.

Despite the horrors of the journey, many of the kids refused to give up. In a Mexican detention center, Nazario met a boy who had tried to reach the U.S. 27 times. He had been robbed and beaten. His girlfriend had been raped. "Tomorrow," he said, "they will send me back to Guatemala. And the next day, I will start on attempt number 28."

Finally, Nazario received a call from a nun in Nuevo Laredo, a Mexican town near the Texas border. "I have a boy here," she said. "I'll put him on the line."

Enrique got on the phone and began to tell his story.

He grew up in Tegucigalpa, the capital of Honduras. His mother, Lourdes, had almost no income. She couldn't even afford pencils for her children to take to school.

Lourdes left home when Enrique was five. She promised to send for him once she had settled in the U.S. But Enrique was devastated. He wondered what he had done wrong to drive his mother off. Every day he asked his grandmother when Lourdes would come home.

A child scavenges in a garbage dump in Tegucigalpa, Honduras. Many of the children who ride the trains across Mexico are migrants from Honduras.

"*Dónde está mi mami?*" he cried, over and over. "Where is my mom?"

In Lourdes's absence, Enrique grew into a troubled teen. He skipped school and got into fights. He hung out with gang members. He sniffed glue to get high.

At night, he'd sit on his grandmother's porch with his girlfriend, Maria Isabel. He'd look up at the stars and tell her about his dream. He wanted to go to America and find his mother.

At 16, Enrique resolved to make the journey. The only information he had was Lourdes's phone number, which he wrote on the waistband of a pair of blue jeans.

Over the next year, he set out seven times. Once, he stayed on the road for 31 days and covered about 1,000 miles. On his sixth trip he made it all the way to the U.S. border in just five days.

Each of Enrique's attempts ended in failure. On one trip he was stopped by *la migra*—the immigration police. The officers stole everything he had—a few crackers, some coins, and some dried-out tortillas. Another time a gang of thugs trapped him on the top of a freight car. They beat him nearly to death before he escaped.

The police caught Enrique several times and deported him to Guatemala. But he refused to give up. On his eighth try he made it all the way to the U.S. border. He was broke but determined to complete his journey.

In May 2000, Nazario went to meet Enrique in Nuevo Laredo. She hung out with him while he begged for money on the streets. She spent two weeks watching him search for a way across the border. Finally she left him to complete his journey by himself. She returned to California to plan her own trip.

Nazario knew what she was getting herself into. The director of a detention center in Texas told her, "For you to do this, you are either stupid or you have a death wish."

Nazario prepared as well as she could. She filled a small backpack with a cell phone, a credit card, toilet paper, cash, and a tape recorder. She also packed a letter from the office of the Mexican president. The letter explained what she was doing. She called it her *carta del oro*, or "golden letter." Its purpose was to keep her out of jail.

When she set out for Tegucigalpa, her husband asked her to make one promise: "Don't jump off moving trains."

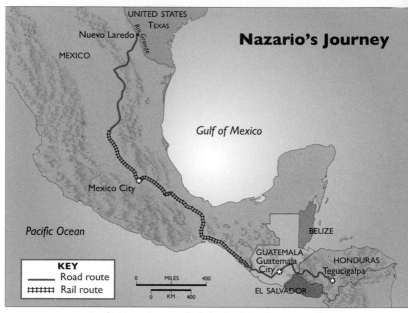

Sonia Nazario traveled the 2,000-mile route of
Enrique's journey—from Tegucigalpa, Honduras,
to Nuevo Laredo, Mexico.

4
The Beast

Nazario arrived in Tegucigalpa hungry for details about Enrique's life. She talked to Maria Isabel. She found the porch where Enrique had revealed his dreams under the stars. And she tried to understand Lourdes's decision to leave home. "When I started this journey, I was judgmental," Nazario admits. "I thought, 'What kind of mother walks away from her children?'"

Tegucigalpa gave her the answer. She watched women pick through garbage to find food for their children. The smell was so bad that she could barely breathe. "Can you imagine knowing that the only way to feed your children—to give them hope for a future—is to walk away from them?" she says.

Nazario left Tegucigalpa the way Enrique did. She rode rickety buses north through Honduras and Guatemala. After 400 miles on the road, she reached the border of Mexico.

She boarded the Train of Death in Chiapas, Mexico's southernmost state. This lawless region is so dangerous that the boys call it *la bestia*, or "the Beast." Drug gangs rule much of Chiapas. Gangsters and thieves beat up defenseless migrants and steal their meager belongings. Corrupt police officers look the other way. Sometimes the police rob the migrants before sending them back across the border.

In Chiapas, Nazario rode with 300 to 400 people crowded on top of the train cars. Many of the riders were kids, some as young as seven. She watched them jump on and off the train to avoid immigration officials. She kept an eye out for gang members and thieves.

For part of her journey, Nazario traveled with a Mexican migrants' rights group. They carried shotguns and AK-47s to fight off the gangsters. Even they protested that the journey was too dangerous for Nazario.

When she traveled alone, Nazario was particularly vulnerable. "Women [on the trains] have an almost 100 percent chance of being raped," she says.

On one occasion, a gangster chased Nazario through the train cars. She escaped by locking herself in a bathroom, crawling out a window, and climbing to the top of the train. "That was probably the scariest moment I faced," she says.

Nazario's most agonizing encounters had little to do with her own safety. She hated to watch children in danger—and always wondered whether she should intervene. As a journalist, Nazario felt her role was to observe. She didn't want to influence the story she was reporting.

A teenager jumps between freight cars on the Train of Death. Accidental deaths are not uncommon.

Still, how could she stand by while kids begged for food or slept in the weeds? She remembered watching Enrique beg on the streets of Nuevo Laredo when she first met him. He had lost his mother's phone number. His grandmother knew the number, but Enrique couldn't afford to call her. "I could have given him my cell phone to call home," Nazario recalls. "But that would have changed their story. It was a very difficult decision. But that's not what a reporter does."

In the end, Nazario decided she would only act if a child's life was in immediate danger. That happened once in Chiapas, when she met a sobbing 12-year-old boy. He had been separated from his friends and arrested. The police were about to deport him to a lawless town. "His odds of being killed were not small," she says. Nazario lent the boy her cell phone to call an uncle for help.

As Nazario rode north from Chiapas, she realized that the dangers of the trip were only part of the story. Enrique and the other migrant kids had a support system to help protect them. On the cars, one teen often stood lookout while the others slept. Boys risked their own safety to pull new riders aboard. Poor villagers along the way chased the train with gifts of food and water.

Acts of kindness like these had kept Enrique alive on his eighth trip. By the time he reached the U.S. border, he told Nazario, he was confident he would make it. He had begun to think of the Train of Death as his "Iron Hope."

Sonia Nazario rides the Train of Death in Mexico.
She rode on seven different trains to find out
what the young immigrants go through as they
try to reach the United States.

Sonia Nazario spent six months retracing Enrique's journey. She survived 16-hour days on the train with little to eat or drink. She interviewed hundreds of people. By the end of her journey, she says, "I was miserable and as exhausted as I'd ever been."

Nazario returned safely to California. She wrote a series of articles about Enrique and the other kids she met on her trip. The stories earned her a Pulitzer Prize, the highest award for a U.S. journalist. She rode the train again in 2003 to do more research. Then she expanded the articles into a book called *Enrique's Journey.*

The book included the end of Enrique's story, which was far from over when Nazario left him in Nuevo Laredo. From Nuevo Laredo, Enrique had to cross the Rio Grande into Texas. He and some other young migrants paid a smuggler to help them cross the river. They waited until dark to hide from border policemen. In a shaky inner tube, Enrique nervously floated on the murky green water. Then he slipped cautiously into the cold river. His teeth chattered as the waves washed him to shore.

The smuggler then led the group on a mad sprint—over a fence, under a pipe, across a bridge and a highway. Enrique arrived, exhausted, at a van that would take him to North Carolina.

Two Central American teenagers silently begin to cross the Rio Grande. The United States is 75 yards away, on the far side of the river.

After seven failed attempts, Enrique's dream had come true. He was reunited with his mother. "He was alone his whole life," Nazario says. "Now he could let out all the love he held inside for years."

Along with the love came a heavy dose of anger. Lourdes had promised to return to her son in Honduras. But she had stayed away for 11 years. Enrique couldn't understand why his mother had abandoned him. "He wanted his mom to get down on her knees and beg for forgiveness," Nazario says. "Lourdes couldn't do that. It would mean that everything she had done was a mistake."

While Enrique was away, Maria Isabel gave birth to their daughter, Jasmin. Now Enrique had the same problem as Lourdes.

Enrique finally reached his mother, Lourdes, after eight attempts. They hadn't seen each other for 11 years.

He was separated from his child in Honduras and could not afford to bring her to the United States.

Maria Isabel struggled to care for Jasmin. She promised her baby that Enrique would send for them. But after four years of waiting, she followed in Enrique's footsteps. She left the child in Honduras and headed north.

Eventually, Enrique, Lourdes, and Maria Isabel moved to Florida. Enrique did construction work and painted houses for a living. The family remained poor, but they were determined not to move back to Honduras.

Telling Enrique's story wasn't easy for Nazario. After coming home, she had nightmares about the Train of Death.

She woke up in a sweat, feeling the tracks rumbling under her.

Eventually the nightmares faded. Today, when Nazario thinks about her journey, she tries to remember the acts of kindness she witnessed.

Most of all, she remembers a moment when the train slowed in the Mexican state of Veracruz. Crowds raced to the tracks, throwing bundles of food to the migrant children. She recalls a 100-year-old woman who had made little bags of tortillas and beans. The woman tossed them into the begging hands of the children on the trains.

"She said to me, 'If I have one tortilla left, I will give half away.'" Nazario says. "That's something I'll never forget."

NATIONAL BESTSELLER

ENRIQUE'S JOURNEY

THE STORY OF A BOY'S DANGEROUS ODYSSEY TO REUNITE WITH HIS MOTHER

Sonia Nazario
Winner of the Pulitzer Prize
With a new Afterword by the author

"Gripping and harrowing . . . a story begging to be told."
The Christian Science Monitor

Sonia Nazario's articles about Enrique won a Pulitzer Prize. She expanded the articles into the best-selling book *Enrique's Journey*.

Sonia Nazario

Born:

Madison, Wisconsin

Grew up:

Kansas and Argentina

Life's work:

Reporting and writing about social issues

Day job:

Journalist and author

Website:

www.enriquesjourney.com

Favorite books:

100 Years of Solitude, Gabriel García Márquez
The Three Musketeers, Alexandre Dumas
Killing Pablo, Mark Bowden
Strength in What Remains, Tracy Kidder
There Are No Children Here, Alex Kotlowitz

Author of:

Enrique's Journey
Numerous articles for the *L.A. Times* and other
publications

She says:

"If you are curious and you want to make this world
better, journalism is an amazing profession. Every day,
I go into other people's worlds and see the joys of their
lives for a while. And then I get to tell their stories. It's a
heck of a ride!"

AT THE TIP OF THE SPEAR

In Afghanistan's Korengal Valley,
American soldiers lived without electricity or
running water. Enemy snipers hid in the hills,
waiting for a chance to kill. Roadside bombs
could shatter a truck in a flash. What kind of
reporter would risk his life to tell that story?

6
Incoming!

Sebastian Junger huddles behind a sand-filled barrier. He is frozen with fear on a hillside in Afghanistan. Bursts of gunfire erupt around him. Soldiers race for position. Between the roar of the guns, Junger hears the men barking information to each other.

"Get his waist! Get his waist!"

"How many rounds you got?!"

Fifty yards beyond the barrier, an unseen enemy is unloading gunfire into the tiny

Sebastian Junger spent five months embedded with American soldiers in the Korengal Valley, the site of some of the fiercest fighting in Afghanistan.

outpost. Two dozen American soldiers are defending their turf—and each other—with their lives.

As a journalist, Junger tries to observe the battle as carefully as he can. But he's got more immediate concerns. Small clots of dirt are jumping from the earth near his feet. It takes a moment for him to realize that he's watching incoming bullets tear up the ground. Bullets, he has learned, move faster than sound. By the time you hear the gunfire, they have already reached their target. Just one unlucky step, and your life could be over—with no warning at all.

As scary as that might be, it's a central fact of combat during wartime. And combat is exactly what Junger wanted to experience. For that, he had come to the right place. It was the summer of 2007, and he had just arrived at the remote American outpost known as Restrepo.

Restrepo was carved into a craggy hillside in the middle of Afghanistan's Korengal Valley. The valley didn't look like much— just a six-mile stretch of rock-and-sand landscape near the Pakistan border.

But it was one of the deadliest places on earth. And it was going to be Junger's home for much of the next year.

Junger had five trips planned to the Korengal Valley. On each trip he would spend a month living with the soldiers there. He would eat army rations, drink army coffee, and sleep on rock-hard army bunks. When the soldiers went on patrol, he would throw on 30 pounds of body armor and march out with them.

Restrepo sits on a ridge above the Korengal Valley, protecting larger U.S. bases below. Restrepo had no electricity or running water and was in one of the most violent spots in Afghanistan.

The payoff, for Junger, was a chance to answer age-old questions: What makes soldiers do what they do? Fighting in a war zone is the world's most dangerous occupation. Why would soldiers volunteer for such a risky job? How do they cope with the constant threat? And could it be that they actually grow to love the terrible thrill of combat?

Junger's companions for the year would be a photographer named Tim Hetherington and the men of Battle Company's Second Platoon. Battle Company was home to 150 of the most combat-hardened troops in the U.S. Army. And their job was one of the toughest. They were supposed to bring the Korengal Valley under the control of the Afghan government. To succeed, they had to gain the trust of village lead-

Members of Second Platoon, Battle Company, relax
at Restrepo. Soldiers stayed at Restrepo for periods
of about two weeks before returning to a larger
base known as the Korengal Outpost.

ers in the area. They also had to clear the valley of several hundred guerrilla fighters from the Islamic extremist group known as the Taliban. The Taliban had ruled Afghanistan before the American invasion of 2001. Now they were fighting to regain control of the country.

Junger had heard Battle Company described as a killing machine. Their commander called them the "tip of the spear," and they had seen more than their share of fighting. Battle Company made up just a tiny fraction of the total troops in Afghanistan. Yet they fought one-fifth of the war's battles.

Nearly 50 American soldiers had been killed in the area. One of them, a well-loved medic named Juan Restrepo, died just before Junger arrived. The outpost had been named in his honor.

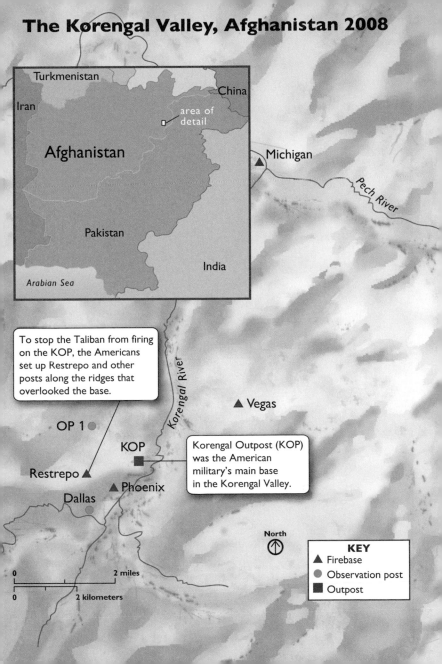

The Korengal Valley, Afghanistan 2008

Turkmenistan

China

Iran

area of detail

Afghanistan

▲ Michigan

Pech River

Pakistan

India

Arabian Sea

To stop the Taliban from firing on the KOP, the Americans set up Restrepo and other posts along the ridges that overlooked the base.

Korengal River

▲ Vegas

OP 1 ●

KOP ■

Korengal Outpost (KOP) was the American military's main base in the Korengal Valley.

Restrepo ▲

Dallas ●

▲ Phoenix

North ⬆

KEY
▲ Firebase
● Observation post
■ Outpost

0   2 miles

0   2 kilometers

The firefight that welcomed Junger to Restrepo almost claimed another life. When it began, a private named Miguel Gutierrez was working on top of one of Restrepo's walls. The first shots snapped past his ear, inches from their target. Reacting instantly, he threw himself off the eight-foot sand barrier. He landed with a thud and broke his ankle on impact.

The fall stranded Gutierrez right in the line of fire. As he squirmed in pain, bullets raked the dirt around him.

In a matter of seconds, a team leader named Aron Hijar stepped into the hail of bullets. With the help of another soldier, he dragged Gutierrez to safety.

Junger, meanwhile, found the courage to leave his hiding place. He stood behind three soldiers while they battered the hill-side with gunfire. After a few minutes, the attack was over. A medic gave Gutierrez a painkiller and examined his leg.

Still reeling from the assault, Junger asked Hijar whether he had hesitated before risking his life to save his friend. "No, he'd do that for me," Hijar said. "Knowing that is the only thing that makes any of this possible."

Junger interviews a survivor of the civil war in Liberia, which claimed the lives of more than 250,000 people. Junger spent several years covering wars in Liberia and other African nations.

7
Drawn to Danger

Junger isn't a soldier. It's not his job to fight wars. So how did he end up ducking bullets on a battlefield in Afghanistan?

Growing up in a wealthy Boston suburb, Junger was a loner. As a teenager, he wandered for hours in the woods. He even excelled at a solitary sport—long-distance running.

When he finished college, he worked as a reporter. But after six years, Junger gave it up and took a job cutting down trees. That's where he found the subject that took him back to journalism: men in dangerous jobs. "Loggers, fishermen, firefighters, oil well drillers," he says. "I wanted to write about them and understand why they risked their lives for a living."

In 1991, Junger was living in Gloucester, Massachusetts, when a fierce storm struck. He watched waves crash against the port. Days later, he read a newspaper article about a fishing boat that had capsized in the storm. Everyone on board was killed. The story fascinated Junger. He spent years reconstructing the last hours of the fisher-men's lives. He wrote a best-selling book about the tragedy called *The Perfect Storm*.

At 31, Junger was hooked on journalism. He didn't have a job with a newspaper or magazine. But he crammed some clothes into a backpack and took off on his own. He flew to Bosnia, an eastern European nation that was in the grip of a bloody civil war.

Junger didn't really know how to report on a war. But he knew he had found his calling. He was part of a community—an elite group of war reporters. And he had a mission: Get close to the action and keep the world informed. "I was completely intoxicated by it," he recalls. "The drug wasn't danger. It was being part of the news machine. That's what I loved."

From Bosnia, Junger flew to the world's most dangerous places. He spent the next few years reporting from war zones in Africa. In Sierra Leone, he was nearly gunned down by rebel fighters. In Liberia, he ran from government soldiers who looted and burned villages.

In Nigeria, gunmen kidnapped Junger and held him hostage for days.

Still he pushed on. Despite all that he had seen, he didn't feel as though he really understood combat. "I still didn't know what it's like to be a soldier," he says.

Junger wanted to spend real time with combat troops. He wanted to get to know them as individuals. He wanted to know what drove them to leave their homes behind and risk their lives on a foreign battlefield. "To understand that, I had to experience it," he says.

In 2007, he decided, the place to do that was Afghanistan. The U.S. had been at war there for six years. American troops invaded in October 2001. The invasion

A soldier in Sarajevo, Bosnia, tries to defend a crowd of civilians from a Serbian sniper. In 1993, Junger traveled to Sarajevo to report on the war between Serbia and Bosnia. The city was under siege for four years.

was a response to the attacks of 9/11, when terrorists hijacked four planes and crashed three of them into the World Trade Center and the Pentagon. Al-Qaeda, the terrorist group that planned the attacks, had its main base in Afghanistan.

At the time of the 9/11 attacks, the Taliban controlled Afghanistan. When the Taliban refused to hand over the leaders of Al-Qaeda, the United States invaded. American forces toppled the Taliban regime within weeks. But some of the Taliban escaped to the countryside and kept fighting. Afghan civilians, many of whom are poor farmers and sheepherders, were caught in the middle. By 2010, more than 1,000 American soldiers and 5,500 of their Afghan allies had died in the war. At least

30,000 Taliban fighters had been killed—
and perhaps as many civilians as well.

When Junger first arrived in the
Korengal, the 30 men of Second Platoon
were just beginning a 15-month tour of
duty in the valley. He settled in, trying
to get to know the soldiers. He knew full
well that some of them might never make
it home.

A machine-gun position at Firebase Phoenix overlooks
the Korengal Valley. Soldiers from Battle Company
spent 15 months at this outpost trying to kill Taliban
fighters and win the support of the local population.

8
Far from Home

Junger arrived at Restrepo on a hot summer day. The position sat on a hillside overlooking the Korengal Outpost, or KOP. The KOP was Battle Company's main base in the valley. The climb from the KOP to Restrepo took two hours in the searing heat. A soldier who wasn't used to the climate vomited on the way up. Another bet $25 that they'd be hit by machine-gun fire before they finished the climb.

They made it safely, and Junger surveyed the scene at the top. The base was little more than a wall of eight-foot sand barriers known as Hescos. Behind the wall, the men of Second Platoon sat on flimsy cots. Many of them wore gym shorts, unlaced combat boots, and no shirts. Cigarettes dangled from their lips.

Living conditions at Restrepo were bleak. The soldiers had no cooked food, running water, or electricity. There was no Internet and no way to contact their friends or family back home. They often went weeks without showers. Sometimes their clothes became so filthy that they had to be burned.

The platoon had no defense against the wilderness. Fleas and tarantulas infested their living quarters. Mountain lions prowled through the camp. Monkeys

A wall of Hescos—steel mesh containers filled with
sand—protect Restrepo.

watched from the trees. One bird made a noise that sounded just like the flight of a rocket-propelled grenade. Every time the soldiers heard it, they flinched.

When Junger first arrived, Battle Company was averaging four or five fire-fights a day. Second Platoon was involved in many of them. In most cases, a sniper fired rounds into the outpost. The soldiers rushed for their weapons. They took cover behind the Hescos and raked the trees with firepower. The attack stopped when the sniper was killed or ran out of ammunition.

Every few days, the platoon went on patrol. They marched out to talk to villagers and search for Taliban fighters. When an attack came, the platoon crouched behind trees or boulders. Adrenaline

Specialist Zachary Boyd (left) helps defend against a
Taliban attack on Restrepo. He had just rushed from
his sleeping quarters in boxer shorts and flip-flops.

pumping, they held off the enemy until they could call in Apache helicopters. The men cheered while the gunships pounded the hillside with massive firepower.

At first, Junger mixed uneasily with the soldiers. The tight-knit group distrusted new arrivals. One mistake by an inexperienced soldier (or journalist) could cost another soldier his life. Junger struggled to keep up on patrol so he wouldn't slow the unit down. He carried his own medical kit in case he was wounded. That way no soldier would have to use up his own supplies.

The platoon had its own bonding rituals, which often made it look like a street gang. Between firefights, the men killed time by picking fights with each other. Once they welcomed a new officer by holding him down and pummeling him in the stomach.

When the shooting started, the soldiers stuck together like family. "One soldier told me that there were people in this platoon who absolutely hated each other," Junger explains. "But every soldier would lay down his life for the guy next to him."

As the summer wore on, the soldiers accepted Junger into their brotherhood. He listened to them without judging them. In return, they opened up, telling him about their lives and the people they'd left behind.

Junger became particularly close to a soldier named Brendan O'Byrne. O'Byrne grew up in Pennsylvania and New Jersey. He had spent much of his young life battling with his father. He was a teenage drinker and pot-smoker. "He had a very rough childhood, and the army kind of saved him," Junger says.

O'Byrne learned discipline from the military. Maybe more importantly, the platoon made him feel wanted. He told Junger the army was full of soldiers like himself—people who had dropped out of school and had struggled to keep jobs. But there on the hill, every man had a vital role. They were in charge of keeping other men alive.

Brendan O'Byrne turns away from the dust kicked up by a Chinook helicopter delivering supplies to Restrepo. This photo was taken by Tim Hetherington, a British photographer who worked with Junger in the Korengal Valley.

An Apache helicopter carries rockets and missiles to attack targets on the ground. Its machine gun can fire 625 rounds a minute and is linked to the pilot's helmet—the gun aims in the direction the pilot turns his head.

9
Death in the Valley

On a cold morning in October, Junger and the men of Second Platoon woke up on a windy hillside. They hadn't shaved in days. Dirt had darkened their faces.

The entire company was on patrol in the most dangerous part of the valley. The four platoons that made up Battle Company were three days into an operation known as Rock Avalanche. It was the biggest action of the year. The goal was to root out Taliban bases located in caves on the ridge above the valley.

The men had been expecting a major attack, but so far there had been no activity. They were just starting to think it wouldn't come at all. Then the gunfire began.

It was total chaos at first. Taliban bullets ripped through branches and thudded into tree trunks. Men scrambled through the forest looking for cover. They tried to return fire, but no one could locate the enemy.

Higher on the ridge, a soldier screamed for a medic. A few men pushed their way up the hill. When they arrived, they found a gunner named Carl Vandenberge soaked in his own blood. He'd been hit in the arm and was bleeding through an artery. "I'm bleeding out, you gotta save me," he pleaded. "I'm dying." Another soldier, Sergeant Kevin Rice, had been hit in the stomach.

Sergeant Larry Rougle was already dead with a bullet through the forehead.

The men quickly tended to the wounded. A soldier stuffed Vandenberge's wound with gauze to slow the bleeding. A medic arrived and gave Vandenberge blood through an IV tube. A minute or two later, Junger noted, and he probably would have died.

With help, Vandenberge and Rice stumbled down the ridge toward safety. They climbed aboard a helicopter to be evacuated. Inside, they lay side by side. Rice reached for Vandenberge's hand, he told Junger later. "We've been through the tough part," he remembered thinking. "We're gonna get help, and we're gonna make it out of this alive."

Apache gunships eventually forced the Taliban fighters to retreat. But by the time the operation ended, five U.S. soldiers were wounded. Five more were dead.

Death was always a possibility in the Korengal. As the company's tour of duty wore on, more and more soldiers had close calls. Most of them had heard bullets snap within inches of their heads. One soldier's helmet stopped a round just before it entered his skull. O'Byrne once leaned over to help an injured Afghan soldier. A bullet hit right where he had been standing.

Everyone had his own way of dealing with the constant threat. Army meals often came with small packs of fruit-flavored candies known as Charms. A superstitious soldier had decided they were bad luck. Every man was expected to throw them away on sight.

Most soldiers simply tried to block the danger out. "There's just places I don't allow my mind to go," O'Byrne told Junger.

Despite the danger, the soldiers seemed to fear one thing even more: boredom. When the bullets started flying, the men were active and useful. It was the waiting that drove them crazy. In the quiet, soldiers were forced to confront their fears. To push away the nightmares, they picked fights with each other. They traded crude jokes about mothers and sisters. "My god," one lieutenant said during a lull, "I wish someone would start shooting at us."

In January, Junger had his own close call. He was returning to the KOP in an armored truck known as a Humvee. Suddenly, an explosion rocked the truck. A sheet of flame washed over the vehicle. Soldiers yelled frantic orders. The Humvee filled with gray smoke. The truck had hit a roadside bomb.

The men were lucky. The bomb exploded under the engine block instead of directly below the cabin. Ten more feet and everyone in the Humvee would have been dead. Instead, Junger and the soldiers he was riding with bolted from the truck. Junger ducked behind its metal hull as the men fired wildly into the forest.

Later, in the relative safety of the base, Junger had trouble calming down. One minute, he wanted to take the next flight home. The next minute, his heart raced with the thrill of the memory. "War is a lot of things," he reflected, "and it's useless to pretend that exciting isn't one of them."

Junger and the soldiers with him escaped with their lives when their Humvee—like this one—hit a roadside bomb. The bomb exploded under the engine block at the front of the vehicle.

Junger and O'Byrne kept in touch after returning from Afghanistan. Here, they're in Massachusetts, preparing to trim tree branches.

10
Coming Home

In the summer of 2008, Battle Company left the excitement and the terrible suffering of battle behind. Their tour of duty ended after 15 months.

The next time Junger saw Brendan O'Byrne was on a New York City street corner. It was a cold winter morning. O'Byrne wore a sweatshirt with the hood pulled over his head. He gripped a cup of coffee in his shivering hands. Junger could see his friend's breath when he coughed.

They had both come a long way from the mountains of Afghanistan.

Junger was writing a book about his experiences in Afghanistan. It would come out in 2010, titled simply *War*. He was also editing a documentary with photographer Tim Hetherington. Titled *Restrepo*, it would be nominated for an Academy Award in 2011.

For months, Junger was haunted by his time in Afghanistan. He had nightmares about firefights and men dying in agony. The nightmares slowly receded. But Junger says he still has unexpected fits of emotion. "I'll start crying for no reason at all," he says.

Many returning soldiers struggle to adjust to life at home. They have trouble explaining the war to friends and family. Some suffer from a condition called post-traumatic stress disorder. They have panic attacks and flashbacks to battles. Many even find themselves craving the excitement of firefights. "Combat is such an adrenaline rush," O'Byrne told Junger in Afghanistan. "I'm worried I'll be looking for that when I get home and if I can't find it, I'll just start … getting in trouble."

O'Byrne was the only member of Battle Company who had left the army. He was having a hard time finding a place in civilian life. He drank too much and got in fights. In the army, O'Byrne had never needed to look for a job, find an apartment, or make a doctor's appointment. The military took care of all that for him. "All he had to do was fight," Junger says. "That's what he was good at."

O'Byrne still thought a lot about his time in Restrepo. O'Byrne missed it, Junger says. He missed everything about it. As he told Junger, if he had the chance, he'd go back in a minute.

Before going to Afghanistan, Junger might have been stunned by O'Byrne's words. How could anyone miss the daily firefights? The sight of men riddled with bullet holes and shrapnel? The unbearable tension of knowing that any moment could be your last on earth?

But as he shared coffee with O'Byrne in the New York City winter, Junger understood. Indeed, he had the same confusing feelings.

"To a combat vet, the civilian world can seem frivolous and dull," Junger says.

"They miss being in a world where everything is important and nothing is taken for granted."

In 2010, the U.S. Army pulled out of the Korengal. After four years of fighting and 50 deaths, military leaders decided that the remote valley no longer had strategic value. It was better just to let it go. Many Battle Company veterans watched YouTube videos of Restrepo being torn down. O'Byrne shrugged when Junger mentioned the pullout.

"What we did up there was for each other," he said. "We fought and we risked our lives and some of us died out there for each other. And you can't take that away. You can't erase that."

Postscript

Like O'Byrne and the rest of Battle Company, Junger understood the bonds forged in battle. In Afghanistan, he had risked his life alongside photographer Tim Hetherington. They both always knew that the next patrol could be their last.

Junger and Hetherington returned safely from the Korengal Valley. But in April 2011, Hetherington was back in the line of fire. He traveled to Libya to document a rebellion against the dictator Muammar Qaddafi.

The news made its way to Junger on April 20. His friend had been caught in a rocket-propelled grenade attack in the city of Misurata. Shrapnel had pierced an artery in his thigh. Hetherington bled to death on the way to a medical clinic.

Junger was devastated. For more than a decade, he had sought out the adrenaline rush of war reporting. He had imagined his own death again and again. But he wasn't ready to lose someone he loved. The experience made him never want to see battle again.

"I now understand the effect of your death on the people you love," Junger told a radio reporter. "And I now realize that even if you don't get killed, every time you go away everyone you love is braced for this…. I'm not doing it anymore, it's over."

Not long after Hetherington's death a Vietnam vet wrote to Junger. His words rang in Junger's head: "The core truth about war is that you lose your brothers. And unfortunately, you now know everything there is to know about war."

Sebastian Junger was photographed in New York City in 2006, the year before he joined the men of Second Platoon in Afghanistan.

Sebastian Junger

Born:

January 17, 1962

Grew up:

Belmont, Massachusetts

Life's work:

Journalist; writer

Website:

www.sebastianjunger.com

Favorite books:

Likes authors with a journalist's sharp eye for detail,
including John McPhee and Joan Didion

Author of:

The Perfect Storm: A True Story of Men Against the Sea
A Death in Belmont
Fire
War

He says:

Junger avoided other books about combat while he was writing
War. "I didn't want to know what other people were doing . . .
I just wanted to do my own thing."

A Conversation with Author
John DiConsiglio

Q *Both Nazario and Junger went to great lengths to tell their stories. What motivated them?*

A Both firmly believe that journalism can make a difference in people's lives. In part, they wanted to raise awareness of issues like immigration and war. By passing on moving stories to the next generation, good journalists can reach out to young people and build their capacity to deal with the important issues of our time.

Q *What does it take to be willing to risk your life for a story?*

A Neither Nazario nor Junger gave much thought to risking their lives. Their spouses were another story. Nazario's husband and Junger's wife were extremely worried.

Q *Would you risk your life for a story?*

A I have occasionally reported from some dangerous locations, like prisons and drug dens. But I never felt like my life was in danger. I wouldn't want to risk my life, mostly because I have a 13-year-old son. Neither Junger nor Nazario have kids. Both said they would think differently about taking risks if they had children at home.

Q *Nazario was reluctant to interfere in the lives of the people she was reporting on. Have you faced a similar ethical issue?*

A In 1999, I reported on the shooting at Columbine High School. I interviewed dozens of kids who escaped the massacre. Many of them had seen their friends gunned down. I debated whether I was intruding on their grief. Fortunately, the kids were remarkably patient with me.

Q *How did you go about researching this book?*

A Most of my research consisted of interviews with Sonia and Sebastian. I talked to them for hours. I also read their books—*Enrique's Journey* and *War*—several times. Then I read countless magazine and newspaper articles. I read just about everything that's ever been written about them. I watched tapes of their TV interviews. By the end of my research, I felt like I knew them pretty well.

What to Read Next

Fiction

Heat, Mike Lupica. (240 pages) *A 12-year-old Cuban immigrant has "the heat" in his pitching arm. But his dream of playing in the Little League World Series is about to be dashed.*

First Crossing: Stories About Teen Immigrants, Donald R. Gallo. (240 pages) *The ten short stories in this collection are about teen immigrants from all over the world.*

Sunrise Over Fallujah, Walter Dean Myers. (320 pages) *A teenager from Harlem learns first-hand how confusing and stressful a war zone can be.*

Illegal, Bettina Restrepo. (256 pages) *Nora, a 15-year-old Mexican girl, and her mother illegally cross into Texas in search of Nora's father.*

Journey of Dreams, Marge Pellegrino. (256 pages) *A Guatemalan family flees the violence in their homeland and makes their way to Arizona.*

Thunder Over Kandahar, Sharon E. McKay. (264 pages) *Two girls in Afghanistan brave numerous dangers as they escape through Taliban territory.*

Nonfiction

Come Back to Afghanistan: A California Teenager's Story, Said Hyder Akbar and Susan Burton. (320 pages) *Akbar returns to Afghanistan. He describes his meetings with warlords and politicians and his visits to palaces and shattered villages.*

Books

War, Sebastian Junger. (304 pages) *Junger tells the story of his time in the Korengal Valley.*

Enrique's Journey, Sonia Nazario. (336 pages) *Nazario describes riding the trains through Central America with young immigrants and the dangers they face at every turn of the journey.*

Films and Videos

The Other Side of Immigration (2010) *This documentary DVD is based on over 700 interviews in Mexican towns in which about half of the population has left for work in the United States.*

National Geographic: Afghanistan Revealed (2001) *This documentary presents the history and people of Afghanistan. It was made just before the 9/11 attacks. Coincidentally, Sebastian Junger appears in the film.*

Websites

http://alt.coxnewsweb.com/palmbeachpost/photos/ accent/tj/tj.html *"Train Jumping: A Desperate Journey" describes the trials and dangers faced by immigrants riding the trains in their attempts to reach the United States.*

http://digitaljournalist.org/issue0304/galloway.html *This site presents "Some Notes on Being a War Correspondent" by Joe Galloway, who reported from war zones for 25 years.*

http://www.cbsnews.com/video/watch/?id=5370231n *CBS war correspondents tell their stories in "Reflections on the War."*

Glossary

Al-Qaeda (AL KYE-duh) *noun* a terrorist network that was founded in Afghanistan in 1998

company (KUHM-puh-nee) *noun* in the U.S. Army, a unit of soldiers made up of three or more platoons

embedded (em-BED-id) *adjective* working as a reporter while under the protection of a military unit

extremist (ek-STREE-mist) *noun* a person who is willing to use violence against people who oppose his or her beliefs

flashback (FLASH-bak) *noun* a vivid re-experience of a stressful or painful event

guerrilla (guh-RIL-uh) *noun* a member of a small group of fighters that often launches surprise attacks against an official army

gunship (GUHN-ship) *noun* a helicopter or plane that flies close to the ground and attacks with rockets and machine guns

intervene (in-tur-VEEN) *verb* to become involved in a situation in order to change what is happening

lieutenant (loo-TEN-uhnt) *noun* a soldier who is typically in charge of a platoon

medic (MED-ik) *noun* someone trained to give medical help during a battle

migrant (MYE-gruhnt) *noun* a person who leaves his or her home country in order to find work

officer (OF-uh-sur) *noun* someone in the armed forces who is in charge of other soldiers

platoon (pluh-TOON) *noun* in the U.S. Army, a unit of about 40 soldiers

post-traumatic stress disorder (POST traw-MAT-ik STRESS diss-OR-dur) *noun* a mental condition that can develop after experiencing a terrifying event. People with PTSD can suffer from anxiety, depression, flashbacks, and substance abuse.

private (PRYE-vit) *noun* a soldier of the lowest rank

refugee (REF-yuh-jee) *noun* a person forced to leave his or her home because of war, persecution, or a natural disaster

regime (ri-ZHEEM) *noun* a government that rules a people for a specific period of time

shrapnel (SHRAP-nuhl) *noun* small pieces of metal scattered by an exploding shell or bomb

sniper (SNYE-pur) *noun* someone who uses a long-range rifle to shoot at people from a hidden place

squad (SKWAHD) *noun* a small group of soldiers

strategic (struh-TEE-jik) *adjective* necessary for the completion of a plan

Taliban (TAL-uh-ban) *noun* an extremist Islamic group

tour of duty (TOOR OV DOO-tee) *noun* the period of time that a soldier serves in a combat zone

---

Metric Conversions

feet to meters: 1 ft is about 0.3 m

miles to kilometers: 1 mi is about 1.6 km

pounds to kilograms: 1 lb is about 0.45 kg

Sources

TRAIN OF DEATH

Author's interview with Sonia Nazario in 2010. (including quotes on pages 4, 16, 22, 23, 26, 30, 31, 35, 37, 38, 40, 42, 43, 45, 48, 51, 105)

"2003 Pulitzer: Feature Photography," Don Bartletti. *Los Angeles Times*, April 2003.

"2009 Yearbook of Immigration Statistics," Office of Immigration Statistics. U.S. Department of Homeland Security, August 2010.

"Argentina 'Dirty War' Military Leader Dies." *Telegraph*, November 9, 2010.

"Blood on the Tracks," Elizabeth Dickinson and Felipe Jácome. *Foreign Policy*, July 23, 2010.

"Central American Migrants Ride 'Train Of Death' To U.S.," Jose Eduardo Mora. *Albion Monitor*, October 6, 2004.

"A Child's Nightmare Ride," Julie Foster. *San Francisco Chronicle*, March 5, 2006.

Enrique's Journey, Sonia Nazario. New York: Random House, 2006. (including quote on page 33)

"Hispanic Trendsetters," Sandra Márquez. *Hispanic Magazine*, 2003. (including quote on page 22)

"The Intervention Dilemma," Susan Paterno. *American Journalism Review*, March 1998.

"Journalist Discusses Teen's Journey to El Norte," Deia De Brito. MissionLocal.org, November 14, 2009.

"'A Just Cause': Central American Migrants and Mexico's Southern Border," Christine Kovic and Patty Kelly. *Houston Catholic Worker*, September–October 2005.

"A Long Journey: Pulitzer Winner Sonia Nazario Shares Her Story," Katie Jenkins-Moses. QuakerCampus.org, November 19, 2009.

"Nazario Champions Stories of Children's Plight," Sandra Kobrin. WomenseNews.org, May 1, 2006.

"One Book, One San Diego 2007." SanDiego.gov.

"A Portrait of Unauthorized Immigrants in the United States," Jeffrey S. Passel and D'Vera Cohn. Pew Hispanic Center, April 14, 2009.

"Prize-Winning Journalist Shares Arduous Journey of Immigrant Children," Mike Williams. *Rice News and Media Relations*, March 14, 2008.

"PW Talks with Sonia Nazario," Marcela Valdes. *Publisher's Weekly*, January 2, 2006. (including quote on page 16)

"Sonia Nazario," Tavis Smiley. PBS.org, March 31, 2006.

"Sonia Nazario Brings 'Enrique's Journey' to Life," Mark Gabrish Conlan. San Diego Independent Media Center, February 28, 2007.

"Spotlight on Legal Immigration to the United States," Jeanne Batalova. Migration Policy Institute, August 2006.

"The Train of Death," Lisa Wong Macabasco. *Mother Jones*, March 3, 2006.

"U.S. Unauthorized Immigration Flows Are Down Sharply Since Mid-Decade," Jeffrey S. Passel and D'Vera Cohn. Pew Hispanic Center, September 1, 2010.

AT THE TIP OF THE SPEAR

Author's interview with Sebastian Junger in 2010. (including quotes on pages 70, 71, 72, 83, 96, 97, 98, 99, 1

"Afghanistan: The Fight Ahead," David Gregory. *Meet the Press*, June 27, 2010.

"American Troops Pull Out of Korengal Valley as Strategy Shifts," Tom Coghlan. *Sunday Times*, April 15, 2010.

"At Veterans Ceremony, Sebastian Junger Pays Tribute to Tim Hetherington," Ted Johnson. WilsherandWashington.com, April 28, 2011. (including quote on page 101)

"Battle Company Is Out There," Elizabeth Rubin. *New York Times*, February 24, 2008.

"Combat High," Sebastian Junger. *Newsweek*, May 10, 2010.

"Documentary *Restrepo* Puts Soldiers' Face on War in Afghanistan," Meg Jones. *Journal Sentinel*, August 18, 2010.

"The Experience of War." *The Charlie Rose Show*, May 26, 2010.

"Fear Itself," Sebastian Junger. *National Geographic Adventure*, March 2007.

"Firebase Phoenix," GlobalSecurity.org.

"HESCO Bastions," Kevlar. *Homemade Defense*, July 30, 2010.

"Hunting for Liberia's Missing Millions," Doreen Carvajal. *New York Times*, May 30, 2010.

"Interview with Sebastian Junger," Robin Young. PRI's *Here and Now*, May 19, 2011. (including quote on page 101)

"Into the Valley of Death," Sebastian Junger. *Vanity Fair*, January 2008.

"Journalist Sebastian Junger." NPR.org, March 7, 2001.

"Junger's *War*: More Than Words," Steven Kurutz. *Wall Street Journal*, May 11, 2010. (including quote on page 96)

"Lifeline," Jon R. Anderson. *Army Times*, 2010.

"Profile: Sebastian Junger." *Independent*, July 29, 2000.

"Restrepo Documentary Follows U.S. Platoon in Afghanistan," Barbara Vancheri. *Pittsburgh Post-Gazette*, September 10, 2010.

SebastianJunger.com.

"Sebastian Junger on the Thrill and Hell of *War*." NPR.org, May 11, 2001.

"Sebastian Junger Talks About Going to *War*," Chris Nashawaty. *Entertainment Weekly*, May 18, 2010.

"Soldier Zachary Boyd Caught Fighting Taleban in Pink Underpants," Sophie Tedmanson. *Times Online*, May 15, 2009.

"Talking About War with Sebastian Junger," Andrew Lubin. PBS.org, October 25, 2010.

"Transitional Justice in the Former Yugoslavia," International Center for Transnational Justice.

"United States' Invasion of Afghanistan." *Ohio History Central*, July 1, 2005.

"U.S. Forces Leave Afghan 'Valley of Death,'" Matthew Rosenberg. *Wall Street Journal*, April 15, 2010.

War, Sebastian Junger. New York: Hatchett Book Group, 2010. (including quotes on pages 57, 64, 67, 88, 89, 90, 92, 97, 99)

"*War*: Sebastian Junger's Hellish Afghanistan Masterwork," Graeme Wood. Salon.com, May 12, 2010.